ILLUSTRATED MAPS OF AMERICA'S

National Parks

MAPS

BY
ABBY LEIGHTON

62 NATIONAL PARKS

GIBBS SMITH
TO ENRICH AND INSPIRE HUMANKIND

First Edition
25 24 23 22 21   5 4

Text © 2021 Abby Leighton
Illustrations © 2021 Abby Leighton

Published by
Gibbs Smith
P.O. Box 667
Layton, Utah 84041

1.800.835.4993 orders
www.gibbs-smith.com

Designed by Abby Leighton
Printed and bound in China

Gibbs Smith books are printed on either recycled, 100% post-
consumer waste, FSC-certified papers or on paper produced
from sustainable PEFC-certified forest/controlled wood source.
Learn more at www.pefc.org.

Library of Congress Control Number: 2020942188
ISBN: 978-1-4236-5378-3

Welcome to AMERICA'S PARKS!

The United States is full of some of the world's most naturally beautiful places. The American idea of a national park has sparked a global movement to protect the natural wonders that surround us.

The first national park in the world was Yellowstone in 1872. It was known to have landscapes and natural wonders that were beyond ordinary life, so the people of the time set it aside, away from any industrialization threats and for the people of America to visit. Since then, we have claimed 62 national parks and hundreds of other protected areas by the National Park Service. The purpose of these parks is to conserve and preserve the exceptional beauty of nature for education, reflection, and enjoyment of life for generations to come.

This book was created to inspire people to explore the limitless opportunities the parks offer. Each and every park in this country has unique characteristics that make it special—attributes that make millions fall in love with them. This book is intended for anyone of any age, whether they're a long-time park lover or just want to learn more of what this country has to offer, to discover, and to appreciate the beauty right in our backyard.

NATIONAL PARK HISTORY:
important figures

MUIR

John Muir [1838-1914]

John Muir was one of the most important advocates for the national parks. Born in Dunbar, Scotland, Muir moved to Wisconsin with his family at a young age. He studied botany and geology at the University of Wisconsin, and after an accident at his job at a factory, he walked from Indiana to Florida, studying botany even more during his journey. He was so inspired by this trip that he sailed to San Francisco to walk to the Sierra Nevada, a trip that would change him forever.

He became nationally famous by writing many published articles about his unconditional surrender to nature. He traveled to various lands which would later become Glacier Bay National Park and Preserve, Mount Rainer National Park, Sequoia National Park, and Petrified Forest National Park. In 1903, Muir camped with president Theodore Roosevelt in Yosemite, which made such an impact on Roosevelt that he declared Yosemite Valley and the Mariposa Grove federally protected.

THEODORE ROOSEVELT
[1858-1919]

Theodore Roosevelt was the 26th president of the United States. He acknowledged the growing corruption of industrialization and sought out a more progressive and liberal point of view.

He was a prominent outdoorsman, he loved hunting, and he worked with John Muir to set up this new idea of national parks.

During his time as president, he created many conservation policies. He founded five national parks, 18 national monuments, and 150 national forests. Along with these accomplishments, he protected many forests and preserved many areas throughout the country. The national parks are one of his greatest legacies.

ROOSEVELT

In 1903, Muir camped with President Theodore Roosevelt in Yosemite, which made such an impact on Roosevelt that he declared Yosemite Valley and the Mariposa Grove federally protected.

GET TO KNOW AMERICA'S PARKS!

There are 62 national parks in America.

Yellowstone was the first on MARCH 1, 1872.

{ Yellowstone has the biggest collection of geysers in the world. }

The world's tallest tree is in Redwood National Park — it towers 379 ft tall.

Crater Lake is the deepest lake in America at 1,949 ft deep.

Landscape Arch in Arches National Park is the 5th longest natural arch in the world.

The hottest temperature recorded on earth was on JULY 10th, 1913 and was 134.1°F

Death Valley National Park is the lowest & hottest place in America.

MAUNA LOA, one of Hawaii's volcanoes, is the most massive volcano in the world!

AMERICA'S NAT

IONAL PARKS

N W E S

frenchman Bay

PORCUPINE
ISLANDS

MOUNT
DESERT
ISLAND

EAGLE
LAKE

BAR HARBOR

CADILLAC
MOUNTAIN

MOUNT DESERT

JORDAN
POND

Mt Desert Narrows

Mt Desert Narrows

LONG
POND

-KEY-

▬ : WATER

▬ : PARK LAND

- - - : TRAILS

═══ : ROADS

ACADIA
National Park

Located on the eastern coastline of
Maine, Acadia National Park covers
49,000 acres of land on Mount Desert
Island. One of its main features is
Cadillac Mountain, the tallest mountain
on the Atlantic coast—the first light
of day in the United States can often be
seen here.

-INFO-

49,075 ACRES

EST. jan 19, 1929

ME

ACADIA

N
W E
S

NATIONAL PARK OF AMERICAN SAMOA

~ I N F O ~
13,500 ACRES
EST. OCT 31, 1988

island of OFU

island of TA'U

FITI'UTA

TA'U

LATA MOUNTAIN

OLOTANIA

LAUFUTI FALLS

SI'U POINT

TUFU POINT

As the only American national park in the Southern Hemisphere, the National Park of American Samoa in the South Pacific protects rainforests, coral reefs, and native culture. This park expands across three islands, and almost one-third of it is oceanic.

POLA ISLAND

VAI'AVA STRAIT

TAFEU COVE

Vatia Bay

MOUNT ALAVA

PAGO PAGO

Pago Pago Harbour

AŪA

Fagasa Bay

~ KEY ~
: PARK LAND
: WATER
- - - : TRAILS
: ROADS

N W E S

INFO
76,629 acres
est. April 12, 1929

N
W E
S

PRIVATE ARCH

Devils Garden trail

LANDSCAPE ARCH

BROKEN ARCH

Klondike Bluffs trail

MARCHING MEN

DELICATE ARCH

Fiery Furnace

arches
National Park

BALANCE ROCK

HAM ROCK

DOUBLE ARCH

Known for over 2,000 natural arches formed in sandstone, Arches National Park is located in the eastern part of Utah. Arches has the world's most dense collection of natural arches.

The Windows

ROCK PINNACLES

PARADE OF ELEPHANTS

NORTH & SOUTH WINDOWS

Petrified Dunes

COURTHOUSE TOWERS

THREE GOSSIPS

Colorado River

UT
ARCHES

♥ MOAB

REUBEN SCOLNICK: THE ORIGINAL ARCH HUNTER

Visiting Arches as a tourist in the 1970's, he went out on a quest to discover as many arches as he could, because no one had been able to find all of them. More than a decade later, he had found hundreds more arches throughout the park.

BADLANDS

SD

Buffalo Gap National Grassland

242,756 ACRES
EST. NOV. 10, 1978

North Unit

Stronghold Unit

RED SHIRT
TABLE OVERLOOK

BADLANDS
WILDERNESS
OVERLOOK

SAGE CREEK
BASIN OVERLOOK

PINNACLES
OVERLOOK

ANCIENT HUNTERS
OVERLOOK

CONATA BASIN OVERLOOK

HOMESTEAD OVERLOOK

Badlands
Wilderness
Area

Conata
Basin

PANORAMA
POINT

key

PARK LAND
ROADS
TRAILS

BADLANDS
NATIONAL PARK

Located in southwestern South Dakota, Badlands National Park
is best known for its unique eroded buttes and the largest
undisturbed grass prairies in America.

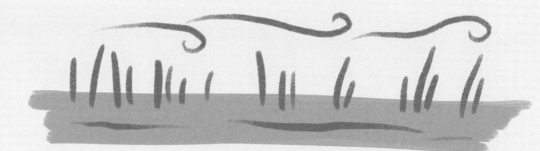

BIG BEND
national park

Bordering Mexico and covering a large portion of the Chihuahuan Desert in Texas, Big Bend protects many natural habitats of the region. It is named after the large bend the Rio Grande river makes throughout the park.

ROSILLOS MOUNTAINS

Dagger mountain

DAGGER FLAT

PAINT GAP HILLS

Roy's Peak

ERNST BASIN

The Window trail

Panther peak

BURRO MESA

Tule mountain

Emory peak

Chilicotal Mountain

CHISOS MOUNTAINS

Dominguez Mountain

Talley Mountain

MESA DE ANGUILA

USA.

USA

Mariscal Mountain

MEXICO

MEXICO

KEY
: WATER
: PARK TERRITORY
: SHALLOWS/ REEFS
: TRAILS
: ROADS

INFO
172,971 ACRES
ESTABLISHED
JUNE 28, 1980
FL
BISCAYNE •

N W E S

SOLDIER KEY

BREWSTER REEF

black point

RAGGED KEYS

STAR REEF

fender point

BOCA CHITA KEY

SANDS KEY

BISCAYNE BAY

ELLIOTT KEY

TRIUMPH REEF

coon point

sea grape point

point adelle

ott point

LONG REEF

billys point

petrel point

HAWK CHANNEL

W. ARSENICKER KEY

ADAMS KEY

BISCAYNE
NATIONAL PARK

MANGROVE KEY

ARSENICKER KEY

RUBICON KEYS

AJAX REEF

LONG ARSENICKER

RED KEY

PORGY KEY

ANNIVERSARY REEF

TOTTEN KEY

E. ARSENICKER

OLD RHODES KEY

PACIFIC REEF

SWAN KEY

ROCKY REEF

BALL BUOY REEF

Located in Southern Florida, Biscayne National Park preserves many barrier reefs in the ocean, which makes up 95 percent of the park. It has four distinct ecosystems: Biscayne Bay, Florida Reef, the coral limestone keys, and the mangrove swamp.

17

Green Mountain

Wilderness Area

Red Rock Canyon

Wilderness Area

WARNER POINT

SUNSET VIEW

DRAGON POINT

CEDAR POINT

CHASM VIEW

PAINTED WALL VIEW

DEVIL'S LOOKOUT

NARROWS VIEW

Mesa Inclinado

BALANCED ROCK VIEW

BIG ISLAND VIEW

PEAKS VIEW

Grizzly Ridge

HIGH POINT

PULPIT ROCK OUTLOOK

Vernal Mesa

KNEELING CAMEL VIEW

GUNNISON POINT

Wilderness Area

Poison Spring Ridge

TOMICHI POINT

Deadhorse Gulch

N W E S

BLACK CANYON
of the
GUNNISON
Ntl. Park
COLORADO, USA

CO

BLACK CANYON OF THE GUNNISON

30,750 acres
established
OCT. 21, 1999

KEY

PARK LAND
WATER
TRAILS
ROADS

Black Canyon of the Gunnison is located in western Colorado and features the Gunnison River running through it. This park covers the most dramatic part of the canyon, and it is named after the fact that the gorge only gets about 33 minutes of sunlight a day!

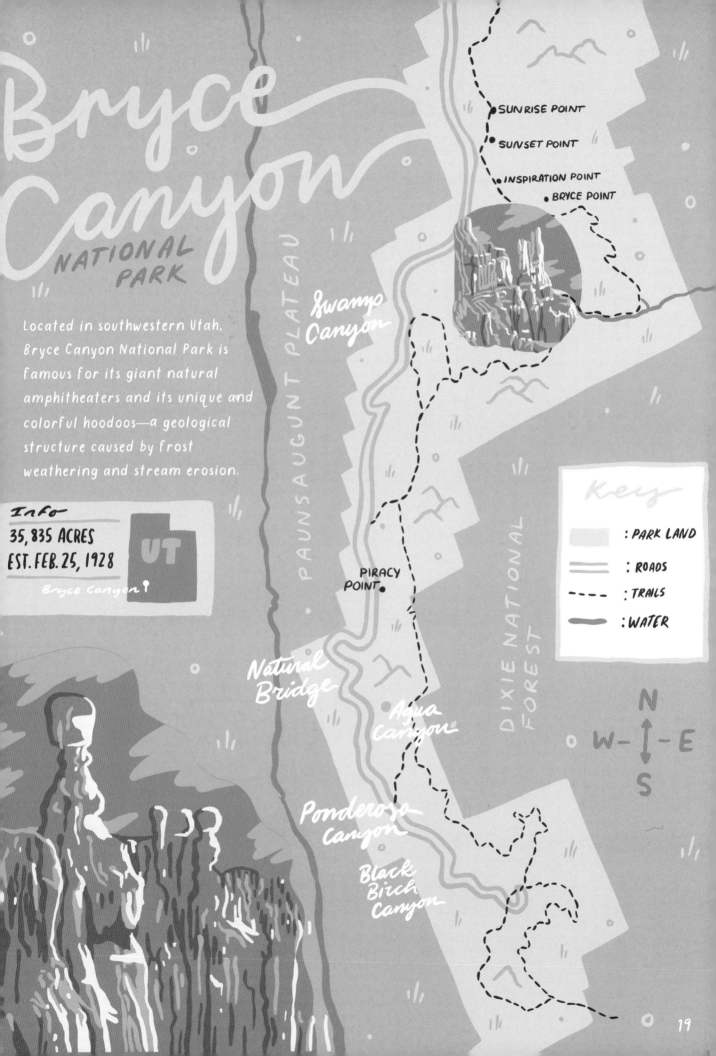

Bryce Canyon

NATIONAL PARK

Located in southwestern Utah, Bryce Canyon National Park is famous for its giant natural amphitheaters and its unique and colorful hoodoos—a geological structure caused by frost weathering and stream erosion.

Info
35,835 ACRES
EST. FEB. 25, 1928

UT

Bryce Canyon

SUNRISE POINT
SUNSET POINT
INSPIRATION POINT
BRYCE POINT

Swamp Canyon

PAUNSAUGUNT PLATEAU

PIRACY POINT

Natural Bridge

Agua Canyon

DIXIE NATIONAL FOREST

Ponderosa Canyon

Black Birch Canyon

Key
: PARK LAND
: ROADS
: TRAILS
: WATER

N
W — E
S

HORSESHOE CANYON UNIT

Known for its buttes, mesas, canyons, and desert atmosphere, Canyonlands National Park covers a portion of southeastern Utah. The park has four different districts: the Maze, the Needles, the Island in the Sky, and the combined rivers (Colorado and Green River).

SHAFER CANYON OVERLOOK

DEAD HORSE POINT

GOOSENECK OVERLOOK

ANTIC OVER

UPHEAVAL DOME • • WHALE ROCK

ISLAND IN THE SKY

HOLEMAN SPRING OVERLOOK

GREEN RIVER

MESA ARCH

GREEN RIVER OVERLOOK

BUCK CANYON OVERLOOK

COLORADO RIVER

GRAND VIEW POINT OVERLOOK

MAZE OVERLOOK

THE MAZE

COLORADO RIVER • OVERLOOK

CONFLUENCE OVERLOOK

BIG SPRING CANYON OVERLOOK

SLICKROCK FOOT

SQUAW FLAT

• WOODEN SHOE OVERLOOK

THE NEEDLES

KEY
- : PARK LAND
- : WATER
- : TRAILS
- : ROADS

Canyonlands
NATIONAL PARK

UT
canyonlands

INFORMATION
337,598 ACRES
ESTABLISHED SEPT. 12, 1964

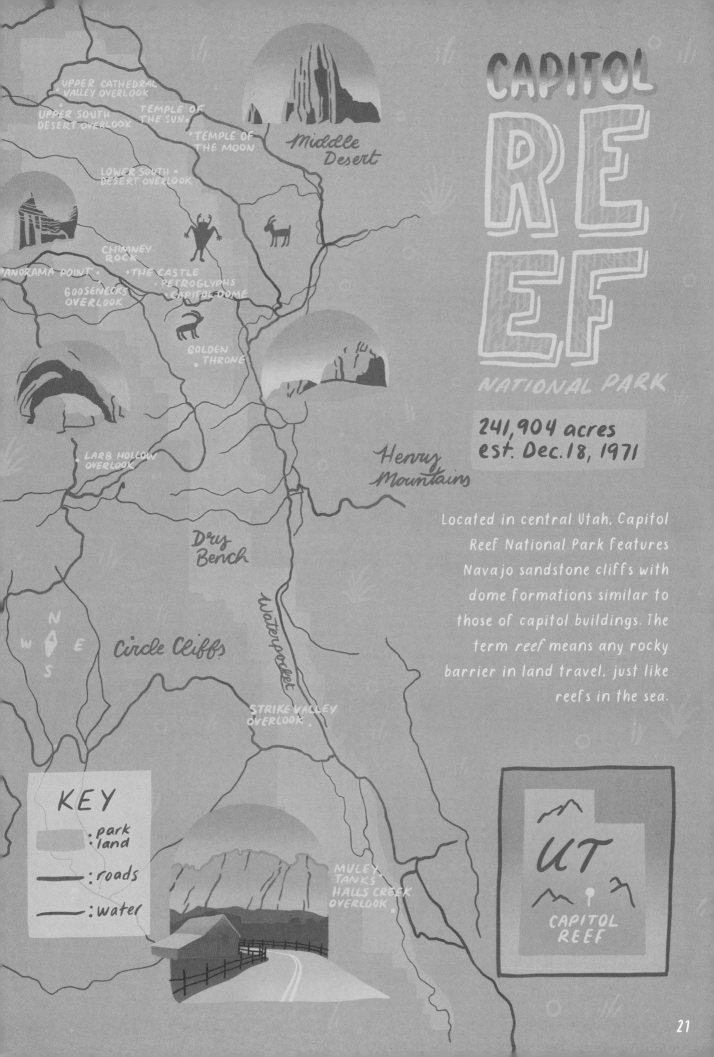

CAPITOL REEF

NATIONAL PARK

241,904 acres
est. Dec. 18, 1971

Located in central Utah, Capitol Reef National Park features Navajo sandstone cliffs with dome formations similar to those of capitol buildings. The term *reef* means any rocky barrier in land travel, just like reefs in the sea.

Middle Desert

Henry Mountains

Dry Bench

Circle Cliffs

Waterpocket

UPPER CATHEDRAL VALLEY OVERLOOK

UPPER SOUTH DESERT OVERLOOK

TEMPLE OF THE SUN

TEMPLE OF THE MOON

LOWER SOUTH DESERT OVERLOOK

CHIMNEY ROCK

PANORAMA POINT

THE CASTLE

PETROGLYPHS

CAPITOL DOME

GOOSENECKS OVERLOOK

GOLDEN THRONE

LARB HOLLOW OVERLOOK

STRIKE VALLEY OVERLOOK

MULEY TANKS HALLS CREEK OVERLOOK

N W E S

KEY
: park land
: roads
: water

UT
CAPITOL REEF

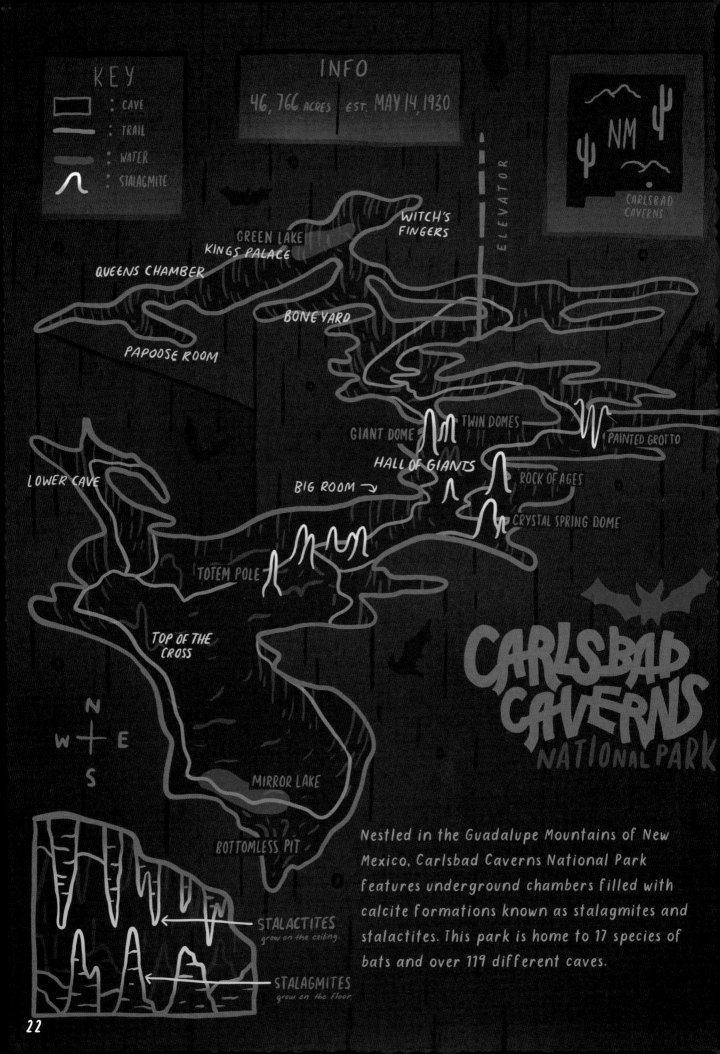

KEY

☐ : CAVE
— : TRAIL
⌒ : WATER
∿ : STALAGMITE

INFO
46,766 ACRES   EST. MAY 14, 1930

NM
CARLSBAD CAVERNS

ELEVATOR

GREEN LAKE
KINGS PALACE
WITCH'S FINGERS

QUEENS CHAMBER

BONEYARD

PAPOOSE ROOM

GIANT DOME   TWIN DOMES   PAINTED GROTTO

HALL OF GIANTS   ROCK OF AGES

LOWER CAVE   BIG ROOM

CRYSTAL SPRING DOME

TOTEM POLE

TOP OF THE CROSS

N
W + E
S

MIRROR LAKE

BOTTOMLESS PIT

CARLSBAD CAVERNS NATIONAL PARK

Nestled in the Guadalupe Mountains of New Mexico, Carlsbad Caverns National Park features underground chambers filled with calcite formations known as stalagmites and stalactites. This park is home to 17 species of bats and over 119 different caves.

STALACTITES
grow on the ceiling.

STALAGMITES
grow on the floor.

SANTA BARBARA

VENTURA

KEY
: MAIN LAND
: ROADS
: PARK LAND
: PRESERVED

N
W E
S

Castle Rock
• Harris Point

SAN MIGUEL

Carrington Point •

West Point •
• Painted Cave

Crook Point
Sandy Point •

SANTA ROSA

SANTA CRUZ

• Skunk Point

• East Point

• San Pedro Point

ANACAPA

CHANNEL ISLANDS
NATIONAL PARK

CA

CHANNEL ISLANDS

Channel Islands National Park includes 5 of the 8 Channel Islands off the coast of southern California. Half the park is in the Pacific Ocean, and the five islands of the park are San Miguel, Santa Rosa, Anacapa, Santa Barbara, and Santa Cruz.

info

249,561 ACRES
EST. MARCH 5, 1980

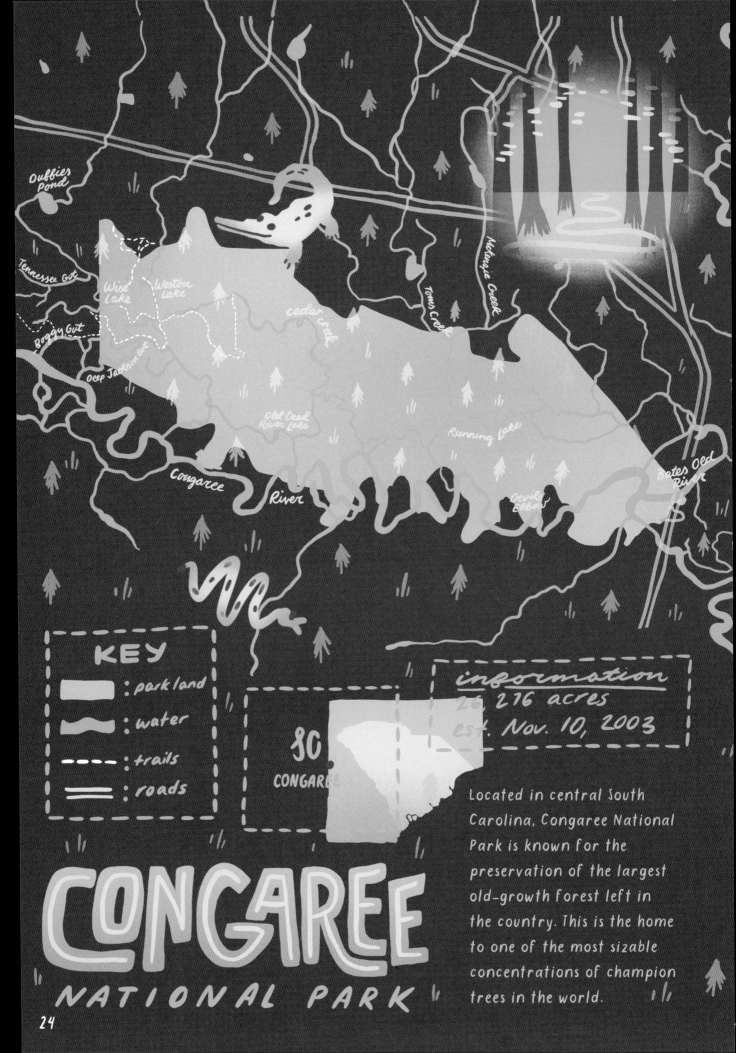

Dubbies Pond

Tennessee Gut

Wise Lake

Weston Lake

Boggy Gut

Deep Jackson Gut

Cedar Creek

McKenzie Creek

Toms Creek

Old Dead River Lake

Running Lake

Congaree River

Devils Elbow

Bates Old River

KEY

: parkland

: water

: trails

: roads

SC
CONGAREE

information
26,276 acres
est. Nov. 10, 2003

Located in central South Carolina, Congaree National Park is known for the preservation of the largest old-growth forest left in the country. This is the home to one of the most sizable concentrations of champion trees in the world.

CONGAREE
NATIONAL PARK

CRATER LAKE

NATIONAL PARK

183,224 ACRES
EST. May 22, 1902

Crater Lake National Park in Oregon is famous for the caldera of Crater Lake, a remnant of the volcano Mount Mazama. A caldera is a large cauldron-like depression that forms after the evacuation of a magma chamber. The lake is 1,949 feet deep, which makes it the deepest lake in the United States.

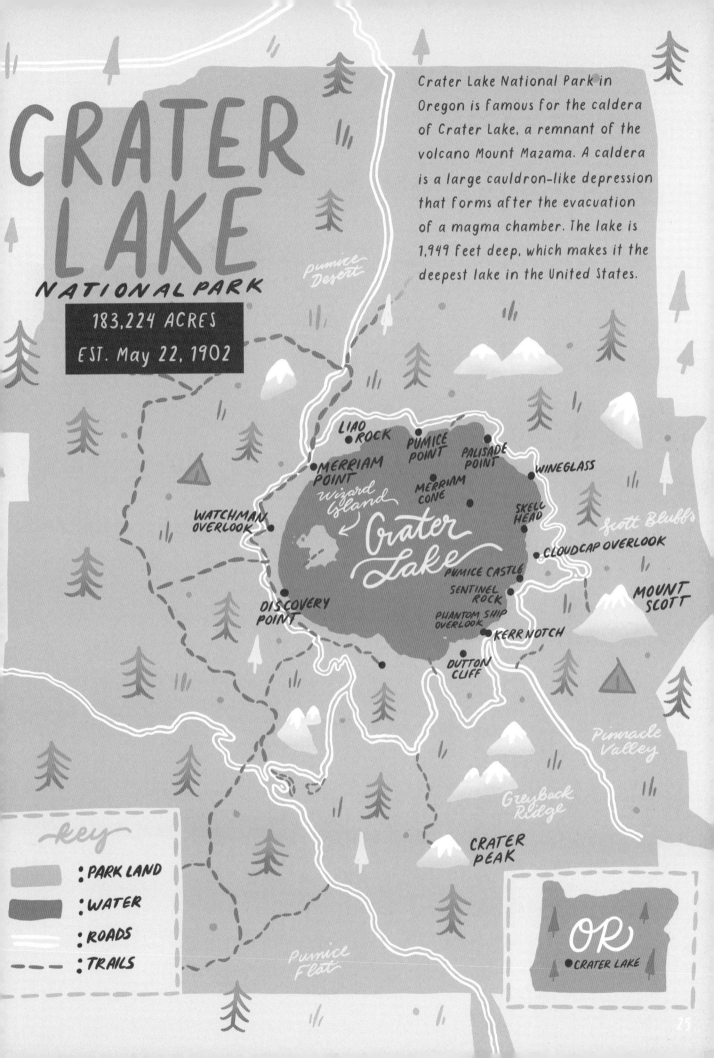

Pumice Desert

LIAO ROCK

PUMICE POINT

PALISADE POINT

WINEGLASS

MERRIAM POINT

MERRIAM CONE

Wizard Island

Crater Lake

SKELL HEAD

Scott Bluffs

WATCHMAN OVERLOOK

CLOUDCAP OVERLOOK

PUMICE CASTLE

MOUNT SCOTT

DISCOVERY POINT

SENTINEL ROCK

PHANTOM SHIP OVERLOOK

KERR NOTCH

DUTTON CLIFF

Pinnacle Valley

Greyback Ridge

CRATER PEAK

Pumice Flat

key

: PARK LAND

: WATER

: ROADS

: TRAILS

OR

CRATER LAKE

Cuyahoga Valley
NATIONAL PARK

Located in Northeastern Ohio, Cuyahoga Valley National Park features the landscape along the Cuyahoga River. This park is unique for its location between two large urban areas near a dense road network and small towns.

VIADUCT PARK

TINKER'S CREEK GORGE

GREAT FALLS

BRIDAL VEIL FALLS

OTTAWA POINT

BRANDYWINE FALLS

BLUE HEN FALLS

STUMPY BASIN

CUYAHOGA VALLEY

OH

Key
- :PARK LAND
- - - - :TRAILS
- ~~~ :WATER
- :ROADS

Info
32,572 ACRES
ESTABLISHED
OCT. 11, 2000

N
W + E
S

DEATH VALLEY
NATIONAL PARK

Eureka Valley Last Chance Range

Grapevine Mountains

•BEATTY

Saline Valley

THE RACETRACK
MESQUITE FLAT DUNES•

•SALT CREEK

LATHROPE WELLS•

Panamint Range

Funeral Mountains

AMARGOSA VALLEY

SKIDOO•

ZABRISKIE POINT

KEY

PARK LAND

ROADS

ARTIST'S DRIVE

DEVIL'S
GOLF COURSE•

DEATH VALLEY JUNCTION

BADWATER• •DANTE'S VIEW

BADWATER BASIN

Black Mountains

INFORMATION
3,373,063 ACRES
EST. OCTOBER 31, 1994

SHOSHONE•

Southern California's Death Valley National Park is famous for its extreme conditions. It is the lowest, hottest, and driest place in America. Its unique features include sand dunes, salt flats, badlands, valleys, and mountains. On July 10, 1913, a world record setting high temperature of 134°F was recorded, and still stands to this day.

DEATH VALLEY

CA

DENALI
NATIONAL PARK
& PRESERVE

Located in Interior Alaska, Denali National Park centers around Mount Denali, the highest mountain in North America. The park protects vast areas of glaciers, tundra, and mountains, and it is larger than the state of New Hampshire!

AK

DENALI

DENALI NATIONAL PRESERVE

4,740,911 ACRES
EST. FEB. 26, 1917

POLYCHROME OVERLOOK

WONDER LAKE

MULDROW GLACIER

ALASKA RANGE

MOUNT DENALI 20,310'

ELDRIDGE GLACIER

RUTH GLACIER

KAHILTNA GLACIER

DENALI NATIONAL PRESERVE

Key

PARK LAND

PRESERVE LAND

GLACIERS

ROADS

DRY TORTUGAS
National Park

Comprised of islands in the Gulf of Mexico near Key West, Dry Tortugas National Park in Florida is the home of vibrant sea life, tropical bird breeding grounds, coral reefs, and shipwrecks.

INFO
64,701 acres
EST. OCT. 26, 1992

FL

📍 DRY TORTUGAS

NORTH COALING DOCK RUINS

Garden Key

MOAT

N

S

FORT JEFFERSON

SOLDIERS' BARRACKS

HARBOR LIGHT

Bush Key

CISTERN

DOCKHOUSE

Dinghy Beach

SWIMMING AREA

SOUTH COALING DOCK RUINS

KEY
WATER
LAND
FORT

Pavilion Key

Wilderness Waterway

Shark Valley

GULF OF MEXICO

Pa-hay-okee Overlook

Key

Park Area
Main Land
Water
Waterway
Roads
Trails

Long Pine Key

Hells Bay

Mud Lake

Nine Mile Pond

Bear Lake

West Lake

Coastal Prairie Trail

Everglades
NATIONAL PARK

FL

Everglades

Located in southern Florida, Everglades National Park protects 27 percent of the original everglades. It is the largest tropical wilderness and the third-largest national park in the United States.

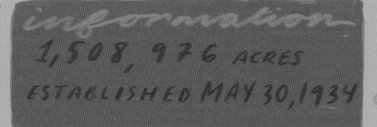

information

1,508,976 ACRES

ESTABLISHED MAY 30, 1934

Gates
OF THE ARCTIC
NATIONAL PARK & PRESERVE

KEY
PARK LAND
WATER

Known as the northernmost national park in America, Gates of the Arctic National Park is located in northern Alaska, and it is the least-visited park in the country. It protects a vast area of the Brooks Mountain Range.

INFO
8,472,506 acres
est. Dec. 2, 1980

W N E S

Brooks Range

Endicott Mountains

NOATAK RIVER

JOHN RIVER

TINAYGUK RIVER

KOYUKUK RIVER

KOBUK RIVER

ARRIGETCH PEAKS

GATEWAY ARCH

MO

GATEWAY ARCH

90 ACRES
EST. FEBRUARY 22, 2018

GATEWAY ARCH
National Park

Located in St. Louis, Missouri, the Gateway Arch is a 630-foot arch that commemorates the Lewis and Clark Expedition and the country's westward expansion.

THE LEWIS & CLARK EXPEDITION
1803-1806

LEWIS TRAIL

FORT CLATSOP

CLARK TRAIL

FORT MANDAN

ST. LOUIS

The Lewis and Clark Expedition from August 1803 to September 1806, also known as the Corps of Discovery Expedition, was the first American expedition to cross the western portion of the United States. It began in Pittsburgh, PA, made its way westward, and passed through the Continental Divide of the Americas to reach the Pacific coast.

MT

CANADA
AMERICA

GOAT HAUNT

MANY GLACIER

ST. MARY

KEY

▭ : PARK
▭ : ROADS
▭ : WATER

CUT BANK

TWO MEDICINE

GLACIER
NATIONAL PARK

Glacier National Park, located in northern Montana, is
famous for its iconic glaciers, lakes, and rocky mountain
peaks. It has over 130 named lakes, 1,000 different species
of plants, and hundreds of animal species.

N
W · E
S

TATAK GLACIER

SAINT ELIAS MOUNTAINS

ALSEK GLACIER

MELBURN GLACIER

GRAND PLATEAU GLACIER

GRAND PACIFIC GLACIER

ALSEK RANGE

TSIRKU GLACIER

CANADA

TAKHINSHA MOUNTAINS

CARROW GLACIER

CRESCENT GLACIER

CHILKAT RANGE

FAIRWEATHER RANGE

FAIRWEATHER GLACIER

BEARTRACK MOUNTAINS

GLACIER BAY

BRADY ICEFIELD

BRADY GLACIER

N E S W

KEY

WATER
MAINLAND
PARK LAND
GLACIERS

AK

GLACIER BAY

GLACIER BAY
NATIONAL PARK & PRESERVE

Located in southeast Alaska, Glacier Bay National Park is only reachable by plane, and it protects over 1,000 different tidewater and terrestrial glaciers.

INFORMATION
3,223,383 ACRES
ESTABLISHED DEC. 2, 1980

WELCOME TO

Grand Canyon

NATIONAL PARK

ARIZONA

TUWEEP

SUPAI

Havasu Falls

Coconino Plateau

key

PARK LAND

WATER

ROADS

The 277-mile-long canyon carved by the Colorado River is the famous wonder of Grand Canyon National Park. Located in northern Arizona, the Grand Canyon is larger than the state of Connecticut and features colorful layers of the Colorado Plateau, exposed by the river. The canyon can be up to 18 miles wide!

Kaibab National Forest

KAIBAB PLATEAU

Painted Desert

North Run

POINT SUBLIME

HAVASUPAI POINT

BRIGHT ANGEL POINT

PIMA POINT

South Run

YAKI POINT

MORAN POINT

DESERT VIEW

GRANDVIEW POINT

TUSAYAN

Kaibab National Forest

GRAND CANYON

NV UT CO

CA NM

AZ

MEXICO

info
1,217,262 ACRES
EST. FEBRUARY 26, 1919

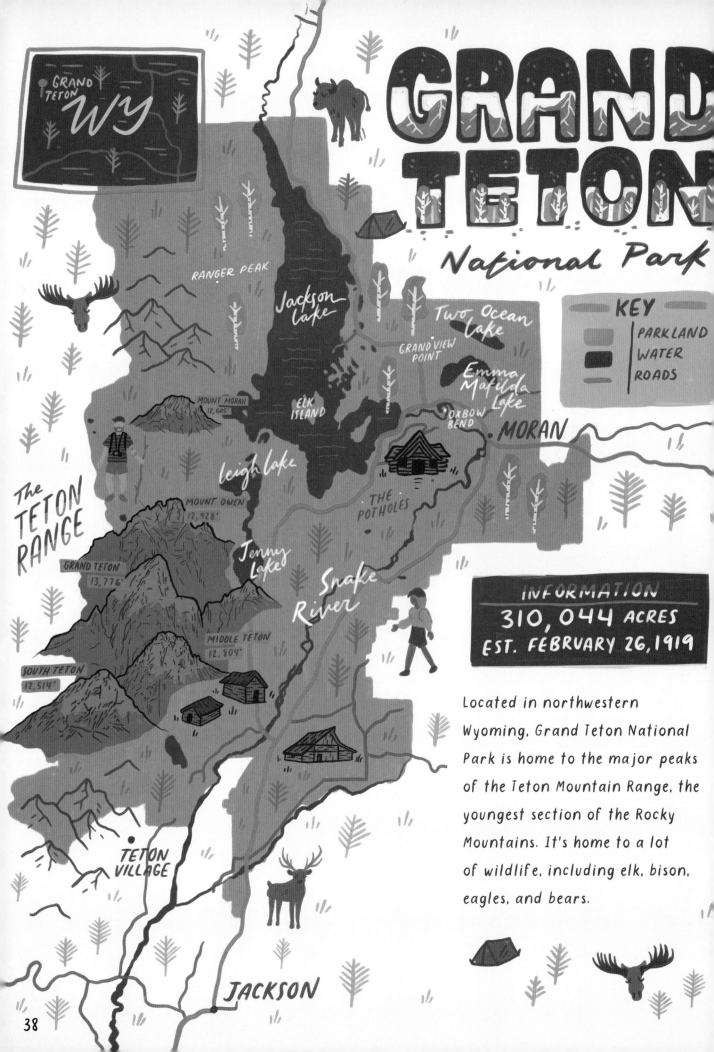

GRAND TETON National Park

GRAND TETON WY

KEY
PARKLAND
WATER
ROADS

RANGER PEAK

Jackson Lake

Two Ocean Lake

GRAND VIEW POINT

Emma Matilda Lake

OXBOW BEND

MORAN

ELK ISLAND

MOUNT MORAN 12,605'

Leigh Lake

THE POTHOLES

The TETON RANGE

MOUNT OWEN 12,928'

Jenny Lake

Snake River

GRAND TETON 13,776'

MIDDLE TETON 12,804'

SOUTH TETON 12,514'

INFORMATION
310,044 ACRES
EST. FEBRUARY 26, 1919

Located in northwestern Wyoming, Grand Teton National Park is home to the major peaks of the Teton Mountain Range, the youngest section of the Rocky Mountains. It's home to a lot of wildlife, including elk, bison, eagles, and bears.

TETON VILLAGE

JACKSON

GREAT BASIN
National Park

Great Basin National Park is located in east-central Nevada, close to the Utah border. Named after the Great Basin region between the Sierra Nevadas and Wasatch Mountains, this dry and rugged park is home to large groves of bristlecone pines, the oldest known nonclonal organisms.

Wheeler Peak

Mather Overlook

Lehman Creek

Lehman Caves

Baker Creek

Granite Basin

Horse Heaven

Bristlecone Pine Grove

Snake Range

Lexington Arch

KEY

PARK
ROADS
TRAILS

NV

GREAT BASIN

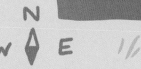

information
77,180 acres
est. OCT. 27, 1986

N W E S

CO
GREAT
SAND
DUNES

149,028 ACRES
EST. SEPT. 24, 2004

SANGRE DE CRISTO MOUNTAINS

KEY
PARK LAND
DUNES
TRAILS
ROADS

DUNEFIELD

WIND

SAND SHEET

WIND

GREAT SAND DUNES

National Park & Preserve

Located in south-central Colorado, Great Sand Dunes National Park is famous for the tallest sand dunes in North America. Many visitors come to this park to try sandboarding, a popular activity of the park.

40

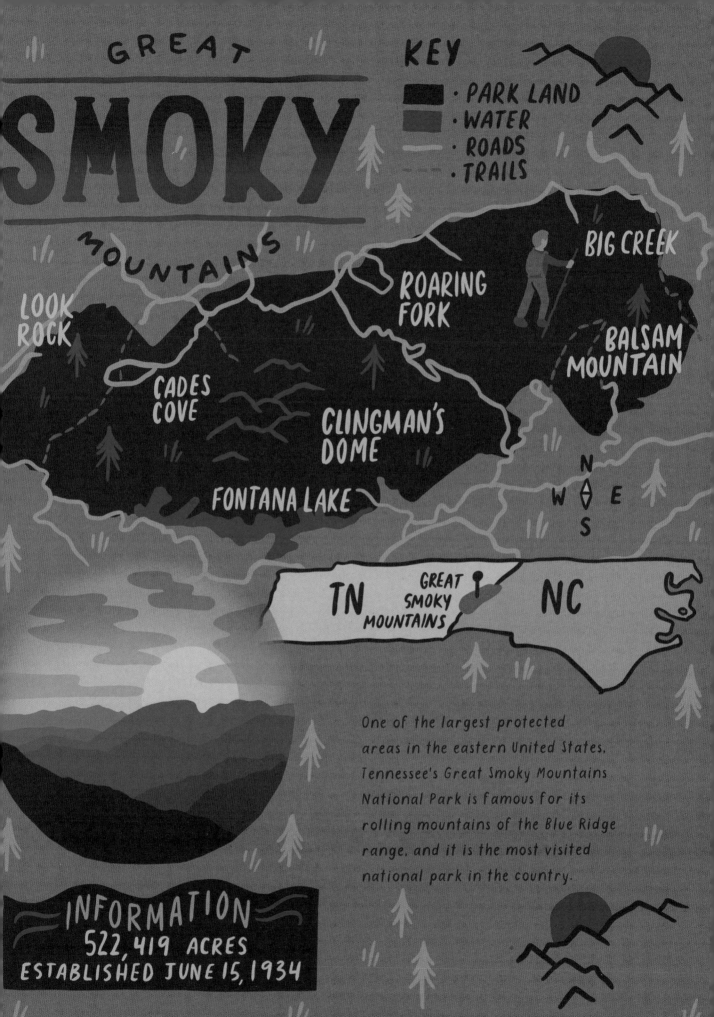

GREAT
SMOKY
MOUNTAINS

KEY
- PARK LAND
- WATER
- ROADS
- TRAILS

LOOK ROCK

ROARING FORK

BIG CREEK

BALSAM MOUNTAIN

CADES COVE

CLINGMAN'S DOME

FONTANA LAKE

N W E S

TN GREAT SMOKY MOUNTAINS NC

One of the largest protected areas in the eastern United States, Tennessee's Great Smoky Mountains National Park is famous for its rolling mountains of the Blue Ridge range, and it is the most visited national park in the country.

INFORMATION
522,419 ACRES
ESTABLISHED JUNE 15, 1934

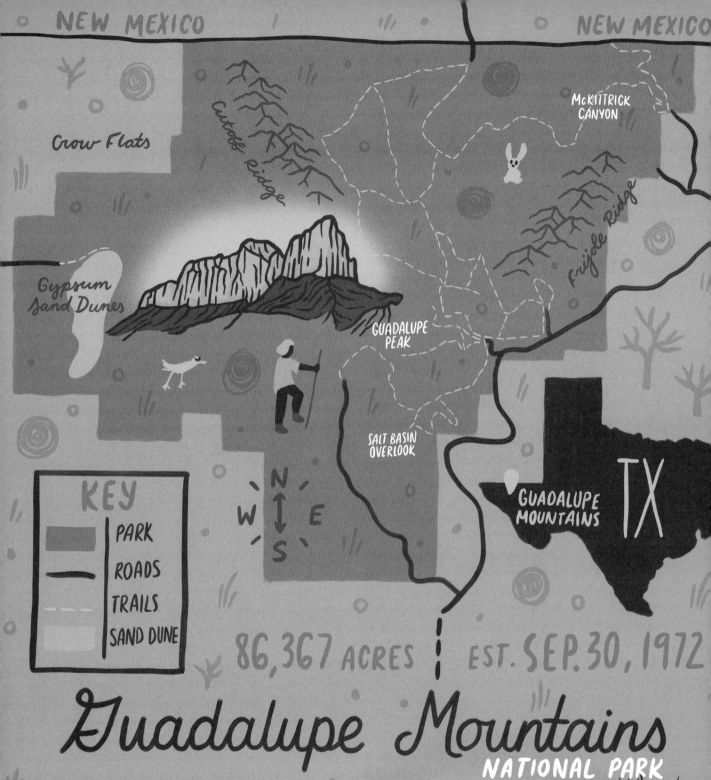

Crow Flats

Cutoff Ridge

McKITTRICK CANYON

Frijole Ridge

Gypsum Sand Dunes

GUADALUPE PEAK

SALT BASIN OVERLOOK

KEY

PARK
ROADS
TRAILS
SAND DUNE

N
W · E
S

GUADALUPE MOUNTAINS

TX

86,367 ACRES | EST. SEP. 30, 1972

Guadalupe Mountains
NATIONAL PARK

Featuring the highest peak in Texas, Guadalupe Mountains National Park is home to unique desert terrains and the world's best example of ancient Permian Age fossil reefs.

KEY

PARK LAND
ROADS
TRAILS
WATER

Island of MAUI

Ieleiwi Overlook

Kalahaku Overlook

KO'OLAU GAP

KAUPŌ GAP

KĪPAHULU VALLEY BIOLOGICAL RESERVE

Waimoku Falls

Falls at Makahiku

Puhilele Point

PACIFIC OCEAN

N
W + E
S

HALEAKALĀ

HI

HALEAKALĀ
NATIONAL PARK

33,264 ACRES
EST. JULY 1, 1961

Located on the island of Maui in Hawaii. Haleakalā National Park is home to the Haleakalā volcano. This park also protects the largest amount of endangered species. Haleakalā is Hawaiian for "house of the sun."

•DEWEY CONE

•LUA POHOLO CRATER

•MAUNA LOA

MAUNA LOA
LOOKOUT

'OLA'A
FOREST

KĪLAUEA

LUA MANU
CRATER

•THURSTON LAVA TUBE

CONE
CRATER

MAUNA
ULU

•MAKAOPUHI
CRATER

HILINA PALI
OVERLOOK

HOLEI S
ARCH

'ĀPUA
POINT

HAWAI'I
VOLCANOES
NATIONAL PARK

HI

ACRES	EST.
323,431	AUGUST 1, 1916

KEY

▬	WATER
▬	LAND
▬	PARK LAND
▬	CRATERS
—	ROADS

Famous for Mauna Loa, the world's largest active
volcano, Hawai'i Volcanoes National Park protects both
Mauna Loa and Kīlauea and offers impressive volcanic
landscapes.

HOT SPRINGS

NATIONAL PARK

As the smallest national park in America, Hot Springs National Park features natural hot springs that flow from the mountains. Inhabitants have used the springs for thousands of years for therapeutic bath purposes.

AR

HOT SPRINGS NAT

KEY

PARK LAND
ROADS
TRAILS

SUGARLOAF MOUNTAIN

City of
HOT
SPRINGS

NORTH MOUNTAIN

HOT SPRINGS MOUNTAIN

WEST MOUNTAIN

INFORMATION

5,550 ACRES
EST. MARCH 4, 1921

INDIANA DUNES

IN

INDIANA
DUNES
NATIONAL PARK

As our second youngest national park, Indiana Dunes covers around 25 miles of the southern shores of Lake Michigan. This park features dunes, wetlands, prairies, and forests.

INFORMATION
15,067 ACRES
EST. FEB. 15, 2019

MOUNT BALDY

GREAT MARSH

DUNE ACRES

WEST BEACH

OGDEN DUNES

INLAND MARSH

HERON ROOKERY

KEY

WATER		PARK LAND
		TRAILS
LAND		ROADS

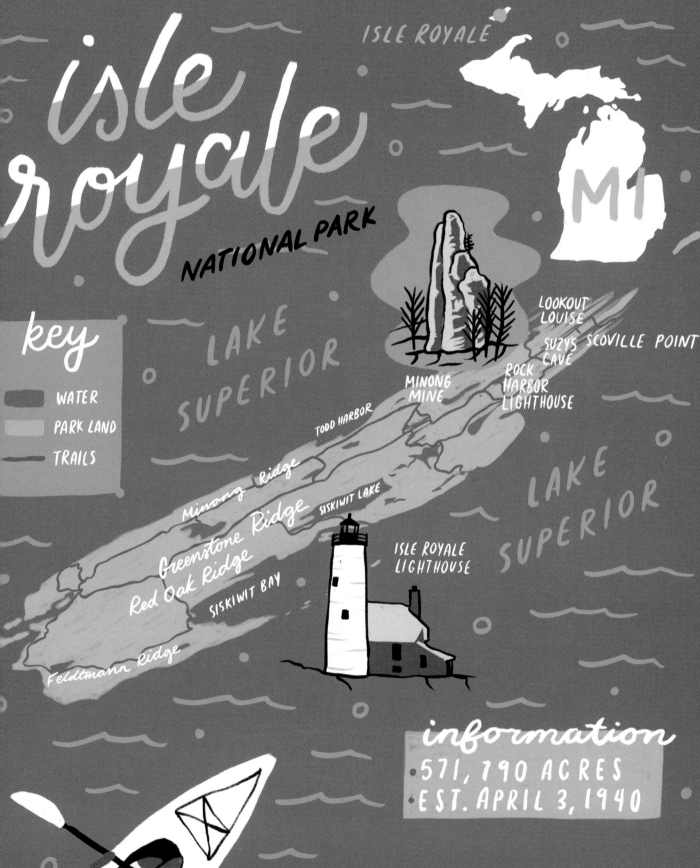

isle royale

NATIONAL PARK

ISLE ROYALE

MI

key

- **WATER**
- **PARK LAND**
- **TRAILS**

LAKE SUPERIOR

LOOKOUT LOUISE

SUZY'S CAVE SCOVILLE POINT

MINONG MINE

ROCK HARBOR LIGHTHOUSE

TODD HARBOR

Minong Ridge

Greenstone Ridge SISKIWIT LAKE

Red Oak Ridge

SISKIWIT BAY

ISLE ROYALE LIGHTHOUSE

LAKE SUPERIOR

Feldtmann Ridge

information
- 571,790 ACRES
- EST. APRIL 3, 1940

Located in Michigan, Isle Royale is home to hundreds of islands in Lake Superior. There are no roads within the park, and it features rocky shorelines, waterways, and shipwrecks.

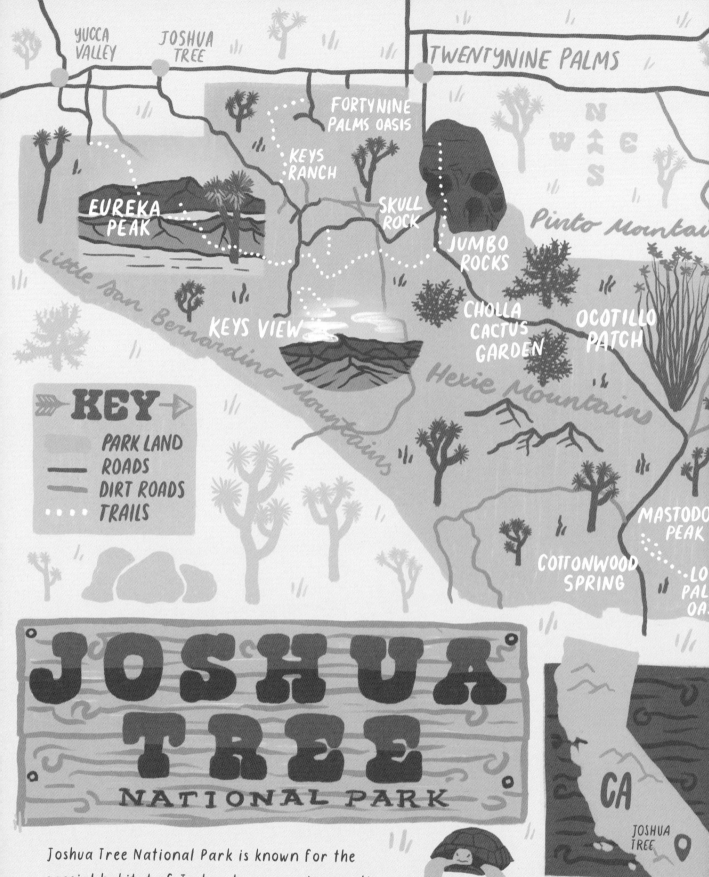

YUCCA VALLEY

JOSHUA TREE

TWENTYNINE PALMS

FORTYNINE PALMS OASIS

KEYS RANCH

EUREKA PEAK

SKULL ROCK

Pinto Mountain

JUMBO ROCKS

KEYS VIEW

CHOLLA CACTUS GARDEN

OCOTILLO PATCH

Little San Bernardino Mountains

Hexie Mountains

KEY
PARK LAND
ROADS
DIRT ROADS
TRAILS

MASTODO PEAK

COTTONWOOD SPRING

LO PAL OA:

JOSHUA TREE
NATIONAL PARK

CA

JOSHUA TREE

Joshua Tree National Park is known for the special habitat of Joshua trees, a unique native plant of the region. Located in southeastern California in the Mojave Desert, Joshua Tree features notable rock formations, clusters of monoliths, and the famous Joshua tree.

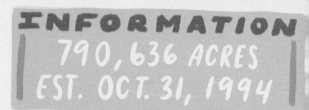

INFORMATION
790,636 ACRES
EST. OCT. 31, 1994

48

RED-TAILED HAWK

JOSHUA TREE

CHOLLA CACTUS

CACTUS WREN

BEAVERTAIL CACTUS

ROADRUNNER

DESERT TORTOISE

TARANTULA

JOSHUA TREE DESERT ECOSYSTEM

KUKAKLEK LAKE

KAMISHAK BAY

NONVIANUK LAKE

LAKE COVILLE

LAKE GROSVENOR

KEY

LAND

PARK LAND

WATER

GLACIERS

TRAILS

ROADS

NAKNEK LAKE

NORTH ARM

DUMPLING MOUNTAIN

LAKE BROOKS

ILIUK ARM

SAVONOSKI

BROOKS FALLS

HOOK GLACIER

THREE FORKS OVERLOOK

VALLEY OF TEN THOUSAND SMOKES

SERPENT TONGUE GLACIER

KEJULIK MOUNTAINS

SHELIKOF STRAIT

Katmai

NATIONAL PARK & PRESERVE

AK

KATMAI

Katmai National Park, located in Alaska, protects the Valley of Ten Thousand Smokes, a century-old ash flow from the eruption of Novarupta. Katmai National Park is also home to Mount Katmai and is well known for their grizzly bear salmon-catching season.

KEY

KEY

WATER

LAND

ICE

PARK
BORDER

HARDING
ICEFIELD

RESURRECTION BAY

AIALIK BAY

HARRIS PENINSULA

HARRIS BAY

KENAI MOUNTAINS

MCCARTY FJORD

AK

KENAI
FJORDS

NUKA
BAY

PYE
ISLANDS

KENAI FJORDS
NATIONAL PARK

INFORMATION
669,984 ACRES
EST. DEC. 2, 1980

Kenai Fjords National Park preserves one of the largest ice fields in the United States, called the Harding Icefield. This field is the source of 38 different glaciers in the park.

Protecting the Kobuk River and three regions of sand dunes, Kobuk Valley National Park is located in northwestern Alaska. These three dunes are the largest dunes in the Arctic. Half a million caribou migrate through the park biannually!

KOBUK VALLEY
NATIONAL PARK

KEY

PARK LAND

WATER

MOUNT ANGAYUKAQSRAQ

BAIRD MOUNTAINS

KOBUK VALLEY

AK

JADE MOUNTAINS

KALLARICHUCK

ONION PORTAGE

AMBLER

GREAT KOBUK SAND DUNES

LITTLE KOBUK SAND DUNES

KIANA

WARING MOUNTAINS

1,750,716 ACRES
EST. DEC. 2, 1980

LAKE CLARK
NATIONAL PARK & PRESERVE

INFORMATION
4,030,015 ACRES
EST. DEC. 2, 1980

The diverse Lake Clark National Park in Alaska is home to two volcanoes, glaciers, rivers, waterfalls, temperate rainforests, tundras, and three mountain ranges. Its millions of acres make it one of the largest parks in the country.

KEY
WATER
LAND
PRESERVE
NATIONAL PARK

THE TUSK

ALASKA RANGE

OLD VILLAGE

TELAQUANA PASS

LAKE CLARK PASS

LAKE CLARK MOUNTAINS

CHIGMIT MOUNTAINS

TWIN LAKES

DICK PROENNEKE'S CABIN

REDOUBT VOLCANO

LAKE CLARK

KONTRASHIBUNA LAKE

PORT ALSWORTH

ALEUTIAN RANGE

AK
LAKE CLARK

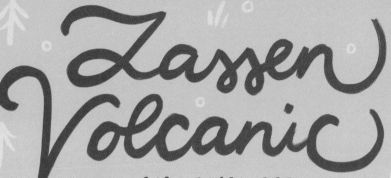

Lassen Volcanic
NATIONAL PARK

INFORMATION
106,452 ACRES
EST. AUG. 9, 1916

BUTTE LAKE

PAINTED DUNES

CINDER CONE

FANTASTIC LAVA BEDS

MANZANITA LAKE

HOT ROCK

CHAOS CRAGS

CLUSTER LAKES

SNAG LAKE

LASSEN PEAK

SUMMIT LAKE

BUMPASS HELL

KINGS CREEK

JUNIPER LAKE

SULPHUR WORKS

DEVILS KITCHEN

FLATIRON RIDGE

KEY
PARK LAND
WATER
TRAILS
ROADS

LASSEN VOLCANIC

CA

Home to the largest lava dome volcano in the world, Lassen Volcanic National Park is located in northern California. Three other types of volcanoes exist here: cinder cone, shield, and composite. These volcanoes create unique landscapes on the surface, such as boiling pools, mud pots, and fumaroles.

MAMMOTH CAVE NATIONAL PARK

BIG WOODS

GREAT ONYX CAVE

CRYSTAL CAVE

HOMESTEAD

BLUFFS

SAL HOLLOW

KEY

PARK LAND
WATER
TRAILS
ROADS

TURNHOLE BEND

KY

MAMMOTH CAVE

Famous for the world's longest cave system, Mammoth Cave National Park is located in Kentucky. Eight bat species, Kentucky cave shrimp, and other unique subterranean wildlife can be found in this park. Above ground, there are many hiking trails, sinkholes, and springs.

INFORMATION
52,830 ACRES
EST. JULY 1, 1941

★ MESA VERDE

MANCOS VALLEY OVERLOOK

PARK POINT OVERLOOK

GEOLOGIC OVERLOOK

Window to the Past

FAIR VIEW

Far View Sites

MESA VERDE

NATIONAL PARK

KEY

PARK LAND
ROADS
TRAILS

STEP HOUSE

Cedar Tree Tower

LONG HOUSE

Kodak House

SPRUCE TREE HOUSE

CLIFF PALACE

Soda Canyon

Pit Houses

BALCONY HOUSE

INFO.
52,485 ACRES
EST. JUNE 29, 1906

Known for over 4,000 archaeological sites of the Puebloan people, Mesa Verde National Park is located in southwestern Colorado, in the Four Corners region. These cliff dwellings were built in the 12th and 13th centuries, and they are the largest archaeological preserve in America.

About 1,400 years ago, the Ancestral Puebloan people thrived in the Four Corners region for several hundred years. They harvested corn, beans, and squash, and they used materials from their environment in their everyday lives. They were excellent basket weavers before they learned to make pottery.

CHENUIS MOUNTAIN

MOUNT
RAINIER

MOUNTAIN
MEADOWS

MOTHER
MOUNTAIN

CRESCENT
MOUNTAIN

Sourdough
Mountains

Ptarmigan
Ridge

EMMONS
VISTA

N
W   E
S

GOAT ISLAND
MOUNTAIN

Klapatche
Ridge

Cowlitz Divide

Emerald
Ridge

PARADISE

MOUNT WOW

Rampart Ridge

Stevens Ridge

Tatoosh Range

GROVE OF
THE PATRIARCHS

KEY

• PARK
  LAND

• ROADS

• TRAILS

• WATER

MOUNT
RAINIER

NATIONAL PARK

INFO

236,381 ACRES

EST. MARCH 2, 1899

Washington's Mount Rainier is an active
stratovolcano covered by some of the country's
biggest glaciers. The nearby town of Paradise is
one of the snowiest places on earth!

KEY

PARK
LAND
WATER
TRAILS
ROADS

Picket Range

Ross Lake

ROSS LAKE OVERLOOK

GORGE CREEK FALLS

DIABLO LAKE

INFO
504,654 ACRES
EST. OCT. 2, 1968

WASHINGTON PASS OVERLOOK

RAINY PASS

NORTH CASCADES
NATIONAL PARK

NORTH CASCADES

WA

North Cascades National Park, located in northern Washington, is home to 312 named glaciers, which is one third of all glaciers in the lower 48 states. It is also known for the largest biodiversity of any American national park, having over 1,630 different species of flora.

OLYMPIC
NATIONAL PARK

KEY
WATER
PARK LAND
ROADS

PORT ANGELES

OZETTE LAKE

LAKE CRESCENT

ELWHA

MORA

FORKS

SOL DUC

HURRICANE RIDGE

HOH RAINFOREST

RUBY BEACH

MOUNT OLYMPUS

KALALOCH

STAIRCASE

N
W E
S

OLYMPIC

WA

922,650 ACRES   EST. JUNE 29, 1938

Olympic National Park is located on the coast of Washington. It has three distinct ecosystems: subalpine forests and meadows, temperate forests, and a rugged Pacific coast.

PETRIFIED FOREST

NATIONAL PARK

Painted Desert

Petrified Forest

AZ

CHINDE POINT

TAWA POINT

KEY
PARK LAND
ROADS
TRAILS

Devil's Playground

NEWSPAPER ROCK

BLUE MESA

Twin Buttes

JASPER FOREST

AGATE BRIDGE

INFORMATION
146,930 ACRES
EST. DEC. 9, 1962

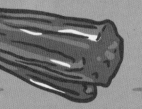

GIANT LOGS

AGATE HOUSE

Well known for the large concentration of petrified wood, Petrified Forest National Park is located in northeastern Arizona. Dating over 225 million years old, the fossils are the essence of this park.

PINNACLES
NATIONAL PARK

Gabilan Range

BALCONIES

Pinnacle Rocks

HIGH PEAKS

BEAR GULCH

PEAKS VIEW

Gabilan Range

KEY

PARK LAND

ROADS

TRAILS

PINNACLES

CA

· INFO ·
26,606 ACRES
EST. JAN. 10, 2013

Pinnacles National Park is located in central California and is named for the remains of an extinct volcano. This park features massive black and gold monoliths, and it is home to the highly endangered California condor. This is one of the few locations left to see these birds in the wild.

RED WOOD

NATIONAL PARK

Located on the northern California coast, Redwood National Park is home to half of the remaining coastal redwood trees. It protects these old-growth forests, pristine coastlines, and a few threatened species, like the tidewater goby, Chinook salmon, northern spotted owl, and Steller's sea lion.

Gold Bluffs

ELK MEADOW

LADY BIRD JOHNSON GROVE TRAIL

ORICK

REDWOOD

CA

REDWOOD CREEK OVERLOOK

TALL TREES GROVE

Bridge Creek Ridge

LYONS RANCH

INFORMATION
138,999 ACRES
EST. OCT. 2, 1968

KEY
LAND ----TRAILS
PARKLAND ROADS
WATER

Rocky Mountain National Park is famous for its rugged mountain peaks of the Rocky Mountains. The Continental Divide runs right through the middle of the park. This park features pristine alpine lakes, mountains, and lots of wildlife.

ROCKY MOUNTAIN

NATIONAL PARK

LULU MOUNTAIN

YPSILON MOUNTAIN

KEY
PARK
LAND
WATER
ROADS

TUNDRA

UPPER BEAVER MEADOWS

ESTES PARK

GREEN MOUNTAIN

BEAR LAKE

EMERALD LAKE

LONGS PEAK

WILD BASIN

INFORMATION
265,461 ACRES
EST. JAN. 26, 1915

ROCKY MOUNTAIN
CO

AZ

SAGUARO

KEY
— PARK
═ ROADS
--- TRAILS

,715 ACRES   EST. **OCT. 14, 1994**

Settled in the Sonoran Desert of Arizona, Saguaro National Park protects the state plant, the saguaro cactus. In addition, it preserves other varieties of cacti, such as the barrel cactus, cholla, and prickly pear.

BAJADA LOOP DRIVE

RED HILLS

SAGUARO NATIONAL PARK

WILDHORSE CANYON

SPUD ROCK
HELENS DOME   REEF ROCK

CACTUS FOREST NORTH

BOX CANYON

MADRONA AREA

Sequoia | Kings Canyon

National Parks

Protecting some of the world's largest trees, Sequoia National Park in California is home to the giant forest sequoias. This forest is home to the world's largest living tree, named General Sherman. In Grant Grove of Kings Canyon National Park, General Grant is the second largest tree in the world!

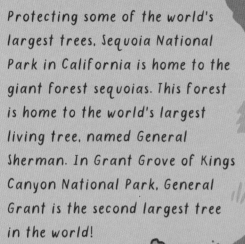

EVOLUTION BASIN

LE CONTE CANYON

ENCHANTED GORGE

Kings Canyon NATIONAL PARK

MONARH DIVIDE

GENERAL GRANT

KINGS CANYON

RAE LAKES

CHARLOTTE LAKE

SPHINX CREST

N
W · E
S

KEY
SEQUOIA
KINGS CANYON
ROADS
TRAILS

CRYSTAL CAVE

·GENERAL SHERMAN TREE

GIANT FOREST

Sequoia NATIONAL PARK

ATWELL GROVE

KERN CANYON

SEQUOIA & KINGS CANYON

CA

GARFIELD GROVE

INFORMATION

SEQUOIA	KINGS CANYON
404,064 ACRES	461,901 ACRES
EST. SEPT. 25, 1890	EST. MAR. 4, 1940

Nestled in a portion of the Blue Ridge Mountains in northern Virginia, Shenandoah National Park features the Shenandoah River and the rolling hills of the Virginia Piedmont. This park is most well known for its Skyline Drive and backcountry camping.

SHENANDOAH

VA

Shenandoah
NATIONAL PARK

BIG MEADOWS

Blue Ridge Mountains

LEWIS MOUNTAIN

LOFT MOUNTAIN

—KEY—
PARK LAND
ROADS

—INFO—
199,173 ACRES
EST. DEC. 26, 1935

THEODORE ROOSEVELT

NATIONAL PARK

Located in western North Dakota, Theodore Roosevelt National Park features different badlands of the region. President Roosevelt came to this region often looking for solitude and the perfect freedom of the West.

KEY

PARK LAND
ROADS
TRAILS

PETRIFIED FOREST

INFORMATION

70,446 ACRES
EST. NOV. 10, 1978

PRAIRIE DOG TOWN

BOICOURT OVERLOOK

RIVER WOODLAND OVERLOOK

NORTH DAKOTA BADLANDS OVERLOOK

ROOSEVELT'S CABIN

MEDORA OVERLOOK

ND

THEODORE ROOSEVELT

Virgin Islands

NATIONAL PARK

KEY
- WATER
- PARK
- ROADS
- ---- TRAILS

ATLANTIC OCEAN

MARY POINT

CINNAMON BAY

MAHO BAY

CRUZ BAY

ISLAND OF ST JOHN

CORAL BAY

EAST END

REEF BAY

SALTPOND BAY

CARIBBEAN SEA

INFO
14,737 ACRES
EST. AUG. 2, 1956

Protecting the tropical pristine beaches and forests of St. John, Virgin Islands National Park features Taino archaeological sites and ruins of sugar plantations from Columbus' time.

RAINY LAKE

BLACK BAY

KABETOGAMA
PENINSULA

CHIEF WOODEN
FROG ISLANDS

KABETOGAMA
LAKE

NAMAKAN
LAKE

YOUR
ISLAND

HOIST BAY

ASH
RIVER

GRASSY
BAY CLIFFS

SAN
POIN
LAK

VOYAGEURS

KEY

NATIONAL
PARK
ROADS
WATER
TRAILS

MN

Voyageurs

NATIONAL PARK

Located in northern Minnesota, Voyageurs National Park protects four lakes near the Canadian border. This park is popular for boaters, kayakers, and canoeists for its exceptional water resources.

WHITE SANDS
NATIONAL PARK

Alkali
Flat

Heart of
the Sands

Interdune
Boardwalk

Lake
Lucero

Dome
Dunes

Parabolic
Dunes

145,762 Acres
EST. DEC. 20, 2019

Originally established as a national monument in
1933, White Sands National Park is now the newest
national park in the system. It is famous for its
pristine white gypsum sand dune fields, which
formed around 10,000 years ago!

NM

WHITE
SANDS

▭ PARK LAND — ROADS ···· TRAILS ▬ WATER

📍 WIND CAVE

LOOKOUT TOWER

RANKIN RIDGE

BOLAND RIDGE

KEY

PARK

ROADS

TRAILS

Red Valley

ELK MOUNTAIN

Prairie Dog Canyon

Windy Point

BISON FLATS

Fossil Ridge

GOBBLER PASS

WIND CAVE

NATIONAL PARK

Known for being the densest and one of the longest cave systems in the world, Wind Cave was established by Teddy Roosevelt in 1903. Above ground, this park protects the largest remaining grass prairie in America.

33,847 ACRES

EST. JANUARY 9, 1903

CAVE FORMATIONS

OF WIND CAVE NATIONAL PARK

FLOWSTONE

Flowstone is formed when calcite water drips down from the ceiling, walls, and along the floor inside a cave.

BOXWORK

Boxwork is created when calcium carbonate dissolved in water crystallizes within the cave's cracks.

Frostwork

Dainty structures of calcite form in spots with higher than average air flow.

CAVE POPCORN

Small rounded calcite balls form where water seeps out of the walls.

DOGTOOTH SPAR

Crystals of calcite form in folds in the limestone in spearlike shapes.

Helictite Bushes

Growing on the floors of caves, these calcite forms are created when water seeps so slowly the calcite deposits against the force of gravity.

Speleothems, also known as cave formations, are naturally forming ornate calcite structures that adorn the cave's interiors. The most famous cave formations of Wind Cave National Park is boxwork. Some of the other common speleothems are flowstone, frostwork, cave popcorn, dogtooth spar, and helictite bushes.

MENTASTA MOUNTAINS
TETLIN LOWLANDS
NUTZOTIN MOUNTAINS

N W E S

WRANGELL MOUNTAINS

CHUGACH MOUNTAINS

GRANITE RANGE

SAINT ELIAS MOUNTAINS

INFORMATION
13.2 MILLION ACRES   EST. DEC. 2, 1980

Wrangell-St. Elias
National Park & Preserve

As the largest national park in the country at over 13.2 million acres, Wrangell-St. Elias takes up a large portion of the south central part of Alaska. It features some of the tallest peaks in North America, with Mount St. Elias as the second highest point on the continent.

AK

WRANGELL-
ST. ELIAS

MAMMOTH HOT
SPRINGS

Gallatin Range

Washburn Range

GRAND CANYON
OF THE YELLOWSTONE

KEY

☐ PARK

── ROADS

〰 WATER

Central Plateau

GRAND PRISMATIC
SPRING

OLD FAITHFUL

Madison Plateau

YELLOWSTONE LAKE

N
W ✦ E
S

Absaroka Range

Pitchstone Plateau

YELLOWSTONE

2,219,790 acres
Est. March 1, 1872

NATIONAL PARK

📍 YELLOWSTONE

WY

Famous for being the oldest and one of the most
popular national parks in the country, Yellowstone
National Park straddles the Wyoming and Montana
border. It features iconic natural landmarks such
as hot springs, geysers, and waterfalls.

YOSEMITE
NATIONAL PARK

Located in the heart of the Sierra Nevada mountain range, Yosemite National Park is iconic for its sheer granite cliffs, monoliths, towering waterfalls, deep glacier-carved valleys, and old-growth forests. It is also the third oldest park in the country and one of the most visited.

HETCH HETCHY RESERVOIR

TUOLUMNE MEADOWS

TENAYA LAKE

YOSEMITE CREEK

EL CAPITAN

HALF DOME

YOSEMITE VALLEY

BRIDALVEIL CREEK

YOSEMITE

CA

MARIPOSA GROVE

INFO
748,436 ACRES
EST. OCT. 1, 1890

KEY
PARK LAND
WATER
ROADS

N W E S

Zion National Park is located in southwestern Utah. Its famous features, such as rock towers, mesas, canyons, and river narrows, are what make up the park. The colorful Navajo Sandstone, eroded by the Virgin River, sets the stage for Zion Canyon.

148,732 ACRES | EST. NOV. 19, 1919

ZION
National Park

Kolob Canyons Viewpoint

Kolob Arch

HOP VALLEY

UPPER KOLOB PLATEAU

Lava Point

LOWER KOLOB PLATEAU

HORSE PASTURE PLATEAU

The Narrows

ORDERVILLE CANYON

Weeping Rock

Angels Landing

Court of the Patriarchs

ZION CANYON

Canyon Overlook

key
- PARK LAND
- TRAILS
- ROADS
- BODIES OF WATER

UT

ZION

Congrats!

You learned about every single national park in the United States. Hopefully, you found a couple of parks you've never heard of and maybe some parks that are now on your bucket list! Good news for us—they're ours to explore and enjoy. But there are a few responsibilities that come with visiting these special places that will help preserve and protect their natural beauty. Here are a few things to keep in mind when you go on your next park adventure:

1. PACK IT IN, PACK IT OUT!

Whatever you bring into the park, be sure to bring it back out with you. It's not cool to litter!

2. Take only pictures

This is protected land, and that includes everything within it. Do not take rocks, plants, signs, or anything else within the park. If you see trash, you can pick that up and leave the land better than you found it!

3. BE PREPARED

The national park climates may not be what you're used to. Make sure to research the weather conditions ahead of time, and be sure to pack accordingly. Bring enough water!

4. STAY ON THE TRAILS

The trails within national parks are there for a reason, and venturing off of them could easily damage the surrounding wildlife. Hike with a buddy, and follow the markers so you don't get lost.

5. RESPECT THE LAND!

These sacred lands are wild and should be as undisturbed as possible. Stay away from wildlife, be mindful of other visitors, and use common sense during your visit.

Abby Leighton visited a national park for the first time in 2014—Zion National Park—and has been inspired ever since. Today she lives in Moab, Utah, designing souvenirs for the national parks and public lands. She has her BFA in illustration from Pratt Institute.